Beautiful
GERMANY

Klaus-Jürgen Vetter (Editor)

BRUCKMANN

CONTENTS

◄◄THE BRANDENBURG GATE – BERLIN. In this gate the good and the bad times are concentrated as at the combustion point of a fire.

◄OBERSTDORF (previous spread), a post Card Idyll. Our picture shows the kind of wanderland that the wanderer will encounter in real life.

"*Mornings are my joy!*
In the quiet hours
I climb the highest peak
and greet you, Germany,
from the depths of my
heart."

Josef von Eichendorff

"Heimweh"

(Homesicknes)

◄ THE KÖHLBRAND BRIDGE which is up to 54m/59yd high and almost 4km/2.4mi long, spans the harbor on the southern banks of the Elbe River in the hanseatic free city of Hamburg. This masterpiece of engineering skill has been the new landmark of Germany's largest city after Berlin since it was opened in the year 1974. Nearby, the Elbtunnel runs deep under the riverbed. Ships from countries all over the world tie up at the quays; sky-high cranes and mountains of containers mark the landscape.

The history of the city "Hammaburg", founded in the 9th century as a seaport, goes back to the 12th century. In 1989 it celebrated the 800th birthday of its harbour, and for centuries it has stood unchallenged at the peak of German seaports. Far more than 10,000 seagoing vessels call at the Hamburg harbour every year, including ocean liners like the Queen Mary 2. The second largest passenger ship in the world often only has the proverbial handbreadth of water under its keel in the Elbe River; the channel is narrow and has many sandbanks. In spite of these actually unfavourable conditions Hamburg has developed into the leading harbour and trading site, the German "gateway to the world".

The city on the Elbe and Alster is of course much more than only a cosmopolitan and active trade and business metropolis. It is also the cultural centre of northern Germany and is one of the most attractive cities between the North Sea and the Alps: with the St. Michaelis Kirche and the Speicherstadt ("Warehouse City"), Planten und Blomen (Botanical Garden), Hagenbeck's Zoo, Jungfernstieg ("Virgin Lane") and Reeperbahn (entertainment district)...

◄◄ FEHMARN. The picturesque harbour Orth on the southern coast of Fehmarn with its brick red former mills and grain stores used to be an important shipping point for agricultural products from the fertile island. Today the harbour which is protected by two long breakwaters is used almost exclusively by sporting boats and a few fishing boats. Windsurfers have excellent conditions on the Orther Reede.

◄◄ SYLT ISLAND. The thatched roof houses of List huddle in the lee of Germany's highest sand dunes. The mountains of sand rise up to over 30m/98ft in the north of Sylt Island and there are still shifting sand dunes in the unique natural landscape of the nearby Listland.

▲ THE FEHMARNSUND BRIDGE spans the kilometre wide sound which separates Fehmarn from the Holstein mainland, as the centre of the so-called Vogelfluglinie between central and northern Europe since 1963. The islanders mockingly refer to the imposing construction as the "largest cloth hanger in the world". It can be seen from far away on the flat unforested island.

◄ BEACHLIFE. The coast of the North and Baltic Seas with their cliffs (here the Red Cliff – Rote Kliff – near Kampen on Sylt Island), marshes, dunes and beautiful beaches are among the most popular German vacation areas. The sun shines longer here than in the interior, but there is often a fresh breeze. The comfortable covered beach chairs provide shelter where you can snuggle up.

◄ NO OTHER PLACE IN GERMANY is as close to the North Pole as the Ellenbogen at 55° north latitude. Two striking lighthouses mark the marram grass-covered tongue of land in the north of Sylt Island. They are the northernmost structures in our country.

▼ HAMBURG AT NIGHT: The city's silhouette is still dominated by high church steeples. With 147m/160yd the steeple of St. Nikolai is the third highest in Germany. The point of the "Michel", what the Hanseatics call the steeple of the Baroque St. Michaelis Kirche, reaches 132m/144yd above the level of the Elbe River. It is the traditional city landmark, and was elevated to bishop's seat in 834.

▼▼ REEPERBAHN. But nighthawks are not attracted by the impressive places of worship, rather by the entertainment and "red light" district St. Pauli.

It bears the name of the apostle Paul. The world famous Reeperbahn is named after the rope makers ("reeper"). It is Hamburg's most sinful street with its bars, nightclubs and sex shows.

▶▼ THE SEA CLOUD, a proud windjammer and today a military yacht, is greeted at the St. Pauli landing with water fountains.

▼▼ THE SUNDAY FISH MARKET, which takes place outdoors early morning on the Großen Elbstraße in the Altona district, is one of many tourist attractions of Hamburg. The market now offers far more than fish;

it covers everything from bananas to carrier pigeons. The salty language of the market criers provides entertainment and there is music for every taste. Every "Sunday until the half past nine bell" (now until half past ten).

▶ "SPEICHERSTADT". No other city in Germany has more bridges than Hamburg: more than 2,500. Many span the fleets, the water channels which run through the unique warehouse city (Speicherstadt). This gem of modern northern German brick architecture was built on an island near the harbor to-wards the end of the 19th century.

◀ **OSTFRIESLAND.** The pretty lighthouse at the edge of the Pilsum tidelands (Pilsumer Watt) in Ostfriesland was built in the 1880s. But because the channel in the lower Ems River (Unterems) silted up it was only in use for a few decades. After restoration the 11m/12yd high tower is now used as an observation platform and registry office. Film fans might recognize it from Otto Waalke's film "Otto – the Extraterrestrial".

◀ **HELGOLAND.** In the centre of the Deutsche Bucht, far away from the coast lies the island Helgoland. With its sandstone red cliffs and the crude remaining arm of a limestone arch called the "Lange Anna", the small island is an outsider among the mostly flat German islands. It has belonged to Germany only since 1890; before that it was British.

◀ **BEST KNOWN LIGHTHOUSE.** The probably best known German lighthouse on the German North Sea coast has stood on the sandbank Westerheversand off the western point of the Eiderstedt Peninsula for about the past 100 years. In good visibility its light can be seen on Helgoland.

▼ **KIEL.** Seafaring, shipbuilding and trade were always very important for Kiel, the state capital of Schleswig-Holstein. In the city on the fjord of the same name and at the locks of the Kiel Canal (Nord-Ostsee-Kanal) the world famous "Kieler Woche" sailing regatta is held every year in June.

◄◄LÜBECK, the time-honoured "Hanseatic Queen", adorns itself with numerous artistic building monuments which were models for countless other structures in the Baltic area. The steeples of the Petrikirche, the Marienkirche and the cathedral tower over the historic city center behind the massive Holstentor built in the 15th century, which is a UNESCO World Heritage site.

◄◄ THE TRAVE RIVER which is divided into several water channels encloses the Altstadt of Lübeck and gives it a unique charm. The Holstenhafen is part of the Stadttrave, the Trave River within the old city. The former carefully restored fire ship Fehmarnbelt is anchored there after decades of service in the North and Baltic Sea.

▲ TIMMENDORF BEACH. On the shores of Lübecker Bucht which separates Holstein and Mecklenburg, bathing beaches line up like pearls on a string. Most of them were made after World War II; Timmendorf Beach with its well-cared for sand beach however looks back on a long tradition as seaside resort.

◄ THE HARBOUR STREET "An der Untertrave", which runs from the Holstentorbrücke downriver along the Trave and the Holstenhafen in Lübeck, is flanked by stately patrician homes. Brick buildings with imposing stepped gable façades, along with some half-timbered houses, make up the picture.

◄ LÜBECK OWES ITS EARLY WEALTH and with that the numerous unique building monuments above all to the "white gold" of the Middle Ages. Salt was transported from the saline city of Lüneburg via the salt road to the harbour on the Trave and loaded onto ships there. The salt stores are reminiscent of this flourishing period, an ensemble of tall brick gabled houses adjoining the Holstentor.

▼ RATZEBURG. Red-brown brick façades and light green roofs toned by copper patina are part of the unmistakable picture of northern German cities, like the Domkirche of the picturesque town of Ratzeburg. The church was completed at the beginning of the 13th century.

►▼ FLENSBURG. The northernmost large city in Germany presses into the innermost corner of the Flensburger Förde. The "city in the valley surrounded by hills" rises from the banks of the fjord and the harbour up to the heights which were formed by ice age glaciers, picturesque with many steps and narrow streets. Flensburg had trading relations worldwide to the West Indies in the past. Its reputation as the German "rum city", which lasted until a few years ago, is reminiscent of this.

▼▼ BREMEN. "We will find something better than death everywhere" – thus the donkey, dog, cat and rooster set off to Bremen to earn their living as city musicians in Grimm's well-known tale. The sculptor Gerhard Marcks has made a beautiful monument to the beastly orchestra in the heart of the old harbour.

▼▼ THE SCHNOOR QUARTER (bottom right). Here in Bremen's oldest residential area the narrow houses stand along narrow streets as if threaded on a string. This might have given the Schnoor (string) Quarter its name.

►THE STATUE OF BREMER ROLAND has adorned the marketplace of the hanseatic city on the Weser since the 15th century. It symbolises the civic pride of an imperial city. The statue is about 10m/11yd tall and chiseled out of Elm mountain limestone. It is the oldest and most important monument in Bremen, but also the largest and most important of the known Roland images.

◄◄ Hannover – the "Grosse Garten" of Herrenhausen on the edge of the state capital of Niedersachsen, was commissioned in 1666 by the duke as a Baroque garden using a Dutch model. A garden theatre, several fountains, stone vases and numerous garden sculptures decorate the expansive garden which is enclosed in a channel. Along with this magnificent example, Hannover has three other great gardens: the Berggarten, Georgengarten and Welfengarten.

◄ The Herrenhäuser Palace was destroyed by bombing strikes in October 1943 during World War II. A gallery building which was completed in 1693 as an orangerie, remains; it is a long elegant building with generous interior stucco decorations.

◄ Hannover – the Holzmarkt. The city on the Leine River, where world famous expositions take place, gives a tranquil historic picture at the Holzmarkt. But the impression is a little deceiving. The half-timbering is only a façade. It covers modern buildings.

▼ Breathtaking view from the dome. The about 100m/109yd high tower dome of the New City Hall (1901–13) offers a breathtaking panoramic view of the Maschteich and the Maschsee, an artificial lake set up in the 1930s – a paradise for water sports –, the Maschpark and the many other green areas which make Hannover a city of parks.

◀◀ ELBMARSCHEN. Comfortable flat hiking trails follow the left-hand bank of the river through the Elbmarschen and the Alte Land outside of the gates of Hamburg. In the spring during cherry and apple blossom time, the largest self-contained orchard region in northern Germany is transformed into a sea of blossoms. The relatively cool climate on the river banks has a decisive advantage: There are fewer bugs and the fruit growers do not need to use as much pesticide.

◀◀ WORPSWEDE AND THE TEUFELSMOOR. Northeast of Bremen lies the austerely beautiful landscape of the Teufelsmoor. At the end of the 19th century the village of Worpswede developed into an artists' colony, where well-known artists like Fritz Mackensen, Heinrich Vogeler or Rainer Maria Rilke lived and worked. Vogeler used the traditional Niedersachsen house as a model for his "Haus im Schuh".

▲ LÜNEBURGER HEIDE. The heidschnucke moorland sheep belongs to the scenery of the Lüneburger Heide just as the hutches of beehives and the ancient juniper bushes do. The contented creatures not only end their lives as a culinary delicacy but are also busy until then as landscape caretakers. They keep down the grass that would otherwise choke out the heather.

◀ SPRUCE AND FIR FORESTS have reduced the heather which blooms dark red in late summer to small patches. The most native heathers can be found in the Hohen Heide around the Wilseder Berg and in the Südheide, here near Celle.

◀ CELLE. The former residence city of Celle on the banks of the Aller is known far beyond Niedersachsen for its castle, horses and orchids, but also for magnificent half-timbered houses, of which there are whole rows preserved in the Altstadt.

▼ HILDESHEIM. The old bishop's seat in the middle of the fertile Hildesheimer Börde has two excellent Romanesque churches, the cathedral and the Michaeliskirche, to whom it owes its entry in the UNESCO World Heritage list. A special highlight is the tall Knochenhaueramtshaus – "Knochenhauer" is an old German word for butcher –, which today houses the city's museum.

▼▼ CHRISTMAS MARKET. In the last weeks of World War II a bombing raid reduced the Hildesheim Altstadt to rubble and ashes. Some of the buildings were rebuilt after the war, including the Knochenhaueramtshaus. Its illuminated windows look down on the Hildesheim Christmas market.

▶▼ TEMPELHAUS. The magnificent gabled façade of the Tempelhaus which was probably built in the first third of the 14th century, also faces the market place. The story of the prodigal son is illustrated on the wall of the upper bay. The Wedekindhaus (1598), stands next to it.

▼▶ HILDESHEIM TOWNHALL (right picture bottom). Arcades, buttresses, arched windows, decorative gables and a façade of ashlar stones are the characteristics of the Hildesheim Rathaus. The history of the stately building goes back to the 13th century, in March of 1945 the Rathaus burned down. Now it has been restored to its former glory.

▶ MARKET FOUNTAIN. Part of the Rathaus façade is visible on the left; the Tempelhaus is in the background, but the market fountain, attested since 1402, stands in the centre. The present form of the fountain dates back to the year 1540. The fountain's basin shows reliefs of Biblical heroes on the side.

◀◀ HANNOVERSCH MÜNDEN. Where the rivers Werra and Fulda kiss... – not only does the Weser River begin its path to the North Sea here, but building monuments worth seeing crowd together on the narrow tongue of land between the two source rivers. Hannoversch Münden is considered to be an architectural treasure chest: with the parish church St. Blasius, the Rathaus in the Weser Renaissance style, the old Werra Bridge, the Welfenschloss and hundreds of magnificent private homes.

▲ STADE (top picture, this page). Rich, but simple northern German-style half-timbering can be found in Stade, the more than 1,000 year-old town at the confluence of the Schwinge and Elbe Rivers. Most of the half-timbered houses, gabled houses with distinctive corbels were built in the second half of the 17th century.

◀ STADE CHANGED ROLES often during its long history; it was in the Hanseatic League, a port city, a fortified city and after the end of the Thirty Years War it even belonged to Sweden for a while. The rows of houses near the harbour impressively reflect the varied history .

▼◀ LÜNEBURG. The Lüneburger Rathaus wears mainly Baroque garments. The largest German rathaus after the one in Lübeck contains structures from the most different stylistic periods. The northern face of the unique ensemble measures a proud 142m/155yd and the imposing façade hides extravagantly furnished rooms.

◄◄ ESSEN, THE METROPOLIS on the Ruhr River, looks back on an eventful history. It was one of the leading industrial centres of Germany for decades. The classicistic Villa Hügel was built around 1870 by the "steel baron" Alfred Krupp in an expansive park above the Baldeneysee as a residence befitting his status.

◄◄ MINER'S COLONY FREUDENBERG. The most joyful thing about the former miner's colony Freudenberg ("mountain of joy") in the Siegerland is the "Alte Flecken", a 17th century town built completely in half-timbering that is almost unchanged. It is an example of unified urban architecture that is unique between the North Sea and the Alps. After a great fire in 1666 the town was rebuilt on the old street layout. Every builder was obliged to strictly follow the old plans.

▲◄ BONN AND BEETHOVEN. A monument to Bonn's most famous son stands in Münster Square of the former nation's capital. The sculptor Ernst Hähnel created the expressive Beethoven monument in 1845, 17 years after the composer's death (he died in Vienna, however). Ludwig van Beethoven, one of the most influential composers of the 19th century, was born in Bonn 75 years earlier.

◄ THE CITY XANTEN on the Lower Rhine is one of the oldest cities in Germany. It was a Roman garrison during the Roman period. This period is revived in the Xanten Archeological Park: with an amphitheatre, baths, sanctuaries, fortifications and not least a stylistically fitting Roman tavern, where meals cooked from ancient recipes are served.

◄ DÜSSELDORF. The daring buildings on the right-hand banks of the Lower Rhine were built almost two millennia later. They transform the Düsseldorf Rheinhafen harbour into a showcase of avantgarde architecture. Behind them the 234m/256yd high Rheinturm rises up.

▼ CARNIVAL IN COLOGNE The fifth season, the "Fastelovend" ("carnival eve"), lasts in Cologne from 11.11. to Ash Wednesday. At that time the Jecken ("fools") of both sexes go wild. For women the "wives' carnival eve", which is celebrated on the Thursday before Shrove Monday, is the absolute high point. Then they take over control of the city on the Rhine for a few hours.

▼▼ THE WDR ARCADES IN COLOGNE actually serve the mundane purpose of preserving and archiving books and other documents that are important for the media. The building that hous-es the archives includes an attractive shopping centre as well as restaurants and cafes.

▼ SWEET MUSEUM. Cologne is rich in important museums. One museum is unusual: the Cologne Chocolate Museum on the Rheinau Peninsula. Its exhibits show the whole history of the sweet temptation.

▼▼ WUPPERTAL (bottom right). In the Bergische Land there are many mountains and rivers, but the valleys are mostly very narrow. The city fathers of Wuppertal made the best of a situation that made traffic difficult and had a suspension railway built at the end of the 19th century. It follows the Wupper River for the most part of its 13km/8mi route. The unusual means of transportation has passed the test of time. Today it's a tourist attraction.

▶ "KÖLNER DOM". Generations have worked for over 600 years on the Cathedral of St. Peter and Mary in Cologne and created a work of superlatives: With its 157m/171yd high towers the Gothic church was the tallest building in the world for centuries. Its western façade is still the largest church façade in the world.

◄◄ AACHEN. In 1978, the Münster in the old city of Aachen was the first German buidling to be added to the UNESCO World Heritage list, along with its treasury. With the Pfalzkapelle in the center the history of the church goes back to the time of Charlemagne. Priceless furnishings were added in every period of history.

◄ BUST OF CHARLEMAGNE. The Aachen Domschatzkammer holds treasures of art of inestimable value. It reflects Aachen's importance as coronation and pilgrimage site until the end of the Middle Ages. Among the countless treasures the Cross of Lothair, the Shrine of Mary, the so-called hunting horn of Charlemagne and the bust of Charlemagne stand out.

◄ CORONATION HALL. Much in Aachen is reminiscent of the Franconian emperor like the market fountain with the image of Charlemagne or the frescoes in the imperial hall of the city hall. They show scenes of the life of the emperor. The huge hall where the coronation feasts and national assemblies were held is one of the most magnificent hall constructions of medieval Germany.

▼◄ TRIER (picture bottom) was founded in the year 16 B.C. by Caesar Augustus and is possibly the oldest city in Germany. It still has numerous historic structures from the Roman period. The Porta Nigra, the "Black Gate" of the Roman fortifications, is foremost. The massive gate has its name from the dark weathered sandstone blocks used to build it towards the end of the 2nd century.

▶ THE FLAT MÜNSTER REGION with its countless large and small waterways is the land of water castles and residences. In the massive Burg Gemen by Borken, the noble family of the same name had their residence. Already at the beginning of the 12th century the name of this romantic fortress which probably developed from an early ring-shaped fortress, appeared in documents. Its light gray walls rise up straight and powerful from the quiet waters: the large square palace from 1411, the archive tower and the ball tower, which got a Baroque roof at the end of the 17th century in an expansive renovation.

▶ THE SCHLOSS NORDKIRCHEN (Nordkirchen castle) fits harmoniously into the Münster park landscape. Unlike other castles of the region, which were often built on ancient foundations, this structure was built new from 1703 to 1734, without any predecessor. Leading architects of the time, like Gottfried Laurenz Pictorius or Johann Conrad Schlaun, created it. The castle which is surrounded by moats and parks, clearly shows the influence of Dutch and French Baroque.

▶▶ MÜNSTER. Many sacred buildings adorn the old city in the centre of the Münster lowlands including St. Paul's cathedral, which is considered to be the most important work of Westphalian architecture and which stands on the foundations of a monastery church built around 800. The Roman Catholic city and market parish church of St. Lamberti on the picturesque Prinzipalmarkt with its arcades and gabled houses were also built on older foundations. The most magnificent and largest parish church in Münster was built in its present Gothic form in the late Middle Ages; the pointed steeple was added in the 19th century.

◄ SPRUCE GREEN, storm blown trees, a white lighthouse, the blue sea in the background – the German Baltic seacoast the way many people know and love it. The picture could have been taken in many places between the Flensburg Förde and the Oderhaff. The striking lighthouse however shows the right place: It is the unmistakable landmark of Hiddensee Island; it stands on Bakenberg in the north of the island and offers a fantastic view from the observation level at 20m/22yd height all the way to the Danish Møn Island.

Hiddensee is Rügen's little sister, Germany's largest island; it is small but fine and more or less the Mecklenburg-Vorpommern's Baltic seacoast in a nutshell. Like all hills along this coast the 72m/236ft high Bakenberg was formed by glaciers. But the coastline was formed long after the glaciers receded when the level of the Baltic Sea rose and partially flooded the ice age landscapes. It created a colourful mosaic of islands, peninsulas, sandbars, bays, inlets and inland lakes, which makes up the special charm of Mecklenburg-Vorpommern's coast. Immediately below the Bakenberg, the Vitter Bodden stretches eastward, a relatively quiet body of water. On the Moränenhöhen and on the western coast there are often stormy winds which whip the few trees and eat away on the cliffs during storm tides. The observation level of the lighthouse is closed for security reasons when the winds reach force 6. The storms are strong, but generally don't last long. The sun shines all the longer however; no other region in Germany gets as much sunshine as the Baltic seacoast.

◀◀ STRALSUND. The beautiful old hanseatic city is located picturesquely on the Strelasund, which separates the island of Rügen from the mainland. The Vorpommeranian city likes to be called the "Venice of the north". The masts of sailing boats sway in the ferry harbor of Stralsund. Behind it in the historic town center, which is on the UNESCO World Heritage list, are the two unlike but massive steeples of the Gothic Nikolaikirche.

◀◀ SCHWERIN CASTLE. Bavaria is not the only place with fairy castles. Schwerin Castle, with its many towers and gables a masterpiece of historicism, also offers an enchanting view. Its location on an island in the center of a wonderful castle garden is idyllic and was redesigned around the middle of the 19th century.

▲◀ STRALSUND – NIKOLAI CHURCH AND TOWN HALL (top picture this page). The steeples of the Nikolaikirche and the filigreed façade of the Stralsund Rathaus merge on the Alte Markt to a unique ensemble of northern German brick building skill. The use of brick was actually a compromise solution since there is little quarriable stone in the northern German lowlands, but this rathaus proves that it's possible to make a virtue out of necessity.

◀ GREIFSWALD. The decorative fronts of the houses along the marketplace of Greifswald draw admiring looks. But the Marienkirche in the background is an introverted construction: almost without decoration on the outside and rather unassuming, but with a magnificent interior.

◀ NOSTALGIC DRAWBRIDGE. The river Ryck flows through the hanseatic city of Greifswald and soon afterwards near the old fishing village Wieck into the innermost point of the Greifswald Bodden. The nostalgic drawbridge of 1886 that was copied from Dutch models crosses the Ryck.

▼ WISMAR. A heavy storm in 1703 caused severe damage to the Nikolaikirche, which is closely surrounded by gabled houses, but the monumental church in the old city of Wismar is still one of the most impressive northern German sacred brick buildings. Its entire splendor can be seen inside; the 37m/40yd high nave is one of the highest in Germany. The storm in 1703 destroyed many works of art, but new ones were acquired to replace them.

▼▼ WARNEMÜNDE. The Alte Strom in the oceanside resort Warnemünde, once the natural mouth of the Warnow into the Baltic Sea, is a colourful site during the summer season today: made up of the many sporting boats in the harbour and the equally charming small, gabled houses lined up.

▼ ROSTOCK (top right picture below) is the largest city in Mecklenburg-Vorpommern and the leading harbour of that state; its old city is located on a rise along the Unterwarnow. Along with modern buildings, its large churches mark the skyline above all: the 117m/128yd high church steeple of St. Petri, always an important landmark for seafarers, the Nikolaikirche and the Gothic Marienkirche built at the beginning of the 15th century.

▼▼ ROSTOCK UNIVERSITY. The traditional main building of the Rostock University presents itself in Neorenaissance style with elaborate terracottas and sgraffito decorations. In front of it on the university square: the "Fountain of the Joy of Life".

▶ FROM THE BEGINNING of the 17th to the end of the 19th century the elegant Dutch Renaissance pavilion on Wismar's Marktplatz provided water for the residents. It literally turned the water supply into "water art".

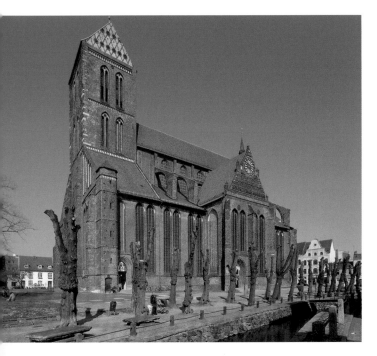

◄◄ Rügen's "Kreidefelsen" — chalk rocks. Normally the layers of the chalk period lie deep below the earth's surface in northern Germany. The light, fossil rich stone only comes to the surface in places, like in salt deposits. On Rügen the layers were forced up by the expanding glaciers of the ice age. The chalk is mixed with ice age deposits and forms high cliffs here with the Baltic Sea persistently gnawing at their feet. Occasionally large parts of the cliff break off.

◄ Hunting castle near Binz. The hunting castle which is located south of Binz on Rügen's 100m/328ft high Tempelberg (tempel mountain) looks more like a medieval castle with its tin covered corner towers, the central tower above the inner courtyard and the bare, unapproachable walls. Duke Wilhelm Malte I. had it built in the first half of the 19th century in the middle of his hunting grounds in Granitz forest, a dense forest rich in game.

◄ Sellin's Sea-Bridge. Every self-respecting seaside resort on the Mecklenburg-Vorpommern coast has a sea-bridge. The pier in the Baltic seaside resort Sellin with its beautifully ornate turn-of-the-century bridgehouse extends about 400m/437yd into the sea. It was only some years ago, that the pier was rebuilt to its original Art Nouveau design. A two storey T-shaped building now houses a restaurant and a number of classy boutiques.

◄ Nostalgic train. Since the end of the 19th century "Racing Roland" ("Der Rasende Roland") steams and spits over Rügen with its locomotive oldtimers and equally old wagons on a narrow gauge track. A biker in good condition can easily outdistance the museum train; but he misses a relaxing ride from Putbus to Binz.

◄◄ POTSDAM's "SCHLOSS SANSSOUCI" ("Carefree Castle") is the centrepoint of an expansive park, which was designed in the 19th century by landscape architect Peter Joseph Lenné and was added to the UNESCO World Heritage list in 1990 along with the buildings of Sanssouci. The summer residence of Prussian kings and German emperors flourished especially under Friedrich II. (1712–1786) also called "the Great".

◄◄ "SCHLOSS SANSSOUCI". The Muschel-saal (mussel hall) is only one of about 200 extravagantly furnished representative and residential rooms in the Neue Palais, which Friedrich II. had built in the 1760s. The artistic monarch often must have felt lonely in the huge residence.

▲◄ CHINESE TEAHOUSE (top picture this page). In the 18th century Europe discovered the art treasures of the Far East. So the ensemble of Sanssouci also has a Chinese teahouse, an individual building whose style betrays how far away the Far East was at that time. Today the teahouse holds a collection of Far East and domestic porcelain.

◄ SANSSOUCI – AERIAL VIEW. An aerial view shows the gigantic dimensions of the Neue Palais in Sanssouci's park. The Late Baroque building under the copper-covered dome and with three wings measures 240m/262yd long; 192 large and 36 small pilasters divide up the façades which are faced with 428 statues.

◄ POTSDAM – HISTORIC CENTRE. The historic centre of Potsdam, the "Versailles of the north", presents itself in middle-class attire, for example in the Dutch Quarter with its pretty brick houses which were built around 1740. The stately gabled house at no. 8 Mittelstraße is reminiscent of the Dutch master builder Jan Bouman (1706–76) who supervised the quarter's construction.

◄◄ BERLIN-MITTE. A place rich in history with the Brandenburg Gate at the Pariser Platz and the street "Unter den Linden", the main street of the old/new capital city of Germany, which leads from the best known landmark in Berlin to the Schloss-platz. In this gate, at the site of Germany's most recent history, the good and the bad times are concentrated as in a focus.

◄ REICHSTAG. The members of parliament meet in the assembly room of the historic Reichstag building in Berlin, grandiose in Italian high Renaissance style, which time has long since passed by. The chancellor's office, which can be seen from sightseeing boats, shows the country from a different, more up-to-date side, without unnecessary pomp.

◄ THE NEW FRIEDRICHSTADTPALAST in Berlin-Mitte has its roots in the decades when the Wall still divided the city on the Spree. It is considered to be Europe's largest revue theatre and it is equipped with most modern stage technology. But the long and varied history of the enter-tainment palace goes back at least 140 years, from a former market hall to the winter quarters of a circus and a large play-house to the production site of popular television programes.

▼ THE HOLOCAUST-MONUMENT south of the Brandenburg Gate of the national capi-tal Berlin is almost as depressing as the reason it was built 60 years after the end of World War II. The sculpture with 2,711 cement stela commemorates the Holo-caust, with its millions of victims during the time of the Nazi regime. Across the Straße des 17. Juni the Soviet monument commemorates the Red Army's dead from the battle for Berlin.

◄◄ DRESDEN. "The Florence of the Elbe" at dusk, in the last light of the setting sun, the grandiose buildings on the Brühlschen Terrasse and the ship's landings illuminated by spotlights. In the background is the Frauenkirche with its unmistakable silhouette. What was once the most important Protestant church in Dresden sank into rubble in February 1945 and was rebuilt after 1993 as a symbol of reconciliation.

◄◄ THE "FÜRSTENZUG" ("procession of dukes") on Dresden Castle is one of the most beautiful sights in the state capital of Sachsen. It was created in the 1870s by Wilhelm Walther and transferred to 25,000 porcelain tiles in 1906. It shows the long history of the ruling house of Wettin.

▲◄ MORITZBURG CASTLE (top picture, this page). August the Strong (1670–1733), elector of Sachsen and King of Poland, was not only a strong, artistic ruler, he was also an avid hunter. He had a grandiose hunting castle built in the middle of the Moritzburger Teiche northwest of Dresden, which is enclosed in a forested park and which holds a collection of hunting trophies.

◄ THE ELBSANDSTEINGEBIRGE ("Elbe sandstone massif") east of Dresden, better known as the "Sächsische Schweiz" ("Swiss Saxony"). The hills with their tabletops, rocky bastions, isolated pillars and deep canyons are less reminiscent of Swiss Alps than of bizarre mountain landscapes across the Atlantic.

◄ THE DRESDEN BRIDGE across the Elbe "Blaues Wunder" ("blue miracle") connects Blasewitz with Loschwitz across the river. The bridge was built in the 1890s, is 200m/218yd long and one of the oldest suspension bridges in Europe, a technical masterpiece at that time.

▼ MEISSEN. Meißen's skyline is certainly one of the most impressive in Germany: Albrechtsburg, the cathedral and the former bishop's castle, which rise up on the Burgberg above the broad Elbe and are visible from far off. But the more than a thousand-year-old city is better known as the site of the first European porcelain manufacture.

▼▼ THE TORHAUS, only one of many monumental structures from the long history of Meißen, which was founded in 928/29 by Heinrich I. as Misni Castle to secure the German feudal rule over the subdued Slavic regions Dale-minzia and Nisan. The building was originally Gothic and was completely changed at the end of the 19th century.

▶▼ LEIPZIG – THE ALTE RATHAUS, a Renaissance structure that was begun around the middle of the 16th century, dominates the market.

▼▼ ST. THOMAS CHURCH – Leipzig is known in the world not only as a city of trade and trade fairs but probably even more as an important site of German musical life. The Late Gothic church after which the famous Thomaner Choir was named is located on the carefully restored Thomaskirchhof (bottom picture). Johann Sebastian Bach worked here for decades as cantor.

▶ THE "ALMA MATER LIPSIENSIS" wears modern clothing today. Yet Leipzig University, which was founded in 1409, is the third oldest in Germany and was always a treasury of the humanities. The Saxons call the university building which was completed in 1975, somewhat disrespectfully the "wisdom tooth". In front of the 140m/153yd giant stands the monument of the philosopher and mathematician Gottfried Wilhelm von Leibniz who was born in Leipzig in 1646.

◄◄ SCHLOSS STOLZENFELS ("Stolzenfeld castle"), which thrones above the Middle Rhine opposite the confluence of the Lahn, is a main work of German Romanticism. The truly proud castle got its present form around the middle of the 19th century as the summer residence of the Prussian king Friedrich Wilhelm IV.

◄ BURG RHEINFELS above St. Goar was once the strongest fortress on the Rhine. It withstood the test of fire in 1692/93, when 28,000 Frenchmen laid siege to the bulwark, which was defended by only 4,000 men. But a century later the occupiers had to surrender to the French without a fight. They blew up the massive castle which has been in ruins since then.

◄ SANKT GOARSHAUSEN in the background nestles up to the foot of steep cliffs which border the Middle Rhine Valley and make it look like a canyon. In the foreground lies Burg Katz (actually "Neu-katzenelnbogen," but in common parlance abbreviated to "Burg Katz") on a promontory high above the river. The strange name of the castle has in fact nothing to do with a "cat," let alone its "elbow" – "Katzenelnbogen" is the name of an old line of Hessian dukes extinct since the end of the 15th century.

▼ THE MIDDLE RHINE VALLEY, today a site on the UNESCO World Heritage list, probably has the highest density of castles in the world. Almost all of the castles are in ruins or were restored recently. Only the Marksburg (picture bottom left) near the old town of Braubach has survived the centuries undamaged.

◄◄ THE WARTBURG near Eisenach has been in German history now for almost 1,000 years. The legendary contest between the Minnesänger is supposed to have taken place here; Saint Elisabeth lived here and (disguised as "Squire George") the Reformer Martin Luther. In 1817 the meetings of the fraternities took place here, which marks a milestone on the road to German unity ...

◄◄ EISENACH – RITES OF SPRING. In spring the people of Eisenach celebrate the "Sommergewinn" (beginning of summer) with many guests, the largest spring festival in Thuringia, when the hated winter is burned in effigy as a strawman. In the summer a historic drama is performed, which is dedicated to Martin Luther, and which lets the Middle Ages come alive through actors and street artists.

▲ THE WARTBURG. The buildings of the Wartburg, which according to legend was founded in 1067, are grouped around two courtyards. The core of the expansive compound from various building epochs includes the knight's house and the official residence with the Luther rooms. Both were reconstructed in the 19th century. The bay window added on the south side in 1872 comes from the Harsdörferschen Haus in Nürnberg.

◄ EISENACH is the birthplace of the composer Johann Sebastian Bach, probably in the house at no. 21 Frauenplan. Today the Bach House holds a collection on the life and work of the Bach family and shows historic musical instruments.

◄ THE WARTBURG FROM THE OUTSIDE. The castle has in fact little room on the Wartberg in the foothills of the Thuringian Forest which run from southeast to northwest. The oldest and most valuable part of the hilltop castle is the Late Romanesque palace with its ground floor arcades in the southeast. The keep rises up above it.

▼ QUEDLINBURG. Hardly any other German city has so many pretty half-timbered houses as Quedlinburg on the northern edge of the Harz Mountains: there are more than 1,000 within the medieval wall, on the Lange Gasse or around the Marktplatz.

▼▼ NAUMBURG. Ekkehard and Uta, two of the twelve limestone founders' figures, which decorate the Naumburger Dom since about the second half of the 13th century.

▶▼ EARLY WEALTH. A fuller's field, beer and wine brought the city near the confluence of Unstrut and Saale early wealth. It can be seen in the stately homes on the Marktplatz, the Stadtkirche St. Wenzel on the south side of the square, but above all in St. Peter and Paul cathedral of Naumburg (early 13th century).

▼▼ WERNIGERODE, the "colourful city at the Harz," has one of the most beautiful German Rathäuser (town hall). Two bay towers with pointed roofs, the double outside staircase as well as the striking ridge turret from 1699 are characteristic of the half-timbered house which was originally built in the 15th century as a playhouse.

▶ KYFFHÄUSER. The small, at the most 500m/1,640ft above sealevel high Kyffhäuser is undoubtedly the one hill around which the most legends have been made between the North Sea and the Alps. One old legend tells of Emperor Friedrich I. Barbarossa, who drowned in a river in Asia Minor and is supposed to have his final resting place here. The imposing sandstone monument was built at the end of the 19th century and shows Emperor Wilhelm I. in the illustrious company of the ruler of the Staufen dynasty.

▶ WITTENBERG. The bronze door of the Schlosskirche in the Luther city of Wittenberg commemorates one of the few really revolutionary upheavals in German history. The reformer is supposed to have nailed his famous 95 theses against the sale of indulgences to the door on October 31, 1517. This was the beginning of the Reformation, which about 100 years later led to the Thirty Years War, the longest war in Germany's history. It left a ruined landscape behind, which marked Germany for decades after the Peace of Westphalia (1648).

▼ "PRAECEPTOR GERMANIAE" – GERMANY'S TEACHER. The statue of Luther's friend and companion Philipp Melanchthon (1497–1560) stands on the expansive marketplace of the Luther city of Wittenberg next to that of Luther. Melanchthon played an important role during the Reformation. He was a highly influential teacher at the Wittenberg university and contributed, among other things, to the systematisation of Reformation thought. In the picture at the bottom the Renaissance Rathaus (left) and the Gothic Stadtkirche St. Marien (right) in the background set striking architectural accents.

▶▶ LUTHERHAUS – THE HOUSE OF LUTHER. Martin Luther moved into the Lutherhaus in Wittenberg in 1508, at that time a "little unknown monastery friar," who taught theology at the renowned Wittenberg University from 1512 on. The stately building with a charming inner courtyard was built in 1504 as the house of the Augustinian monks. Today it houses a museum on the life and work of the reformer.

◄◄ COCHEM. The core of the Reichsburg which thrones over the idyllic wine village of Cochem and the Moselle Valley, is almost 1,000 years old. The count palatine Ezzo of Aachen had it built anno 1027. The lower storey of the massive keep comes from the first construction period. At the end of the 17th century French troops reduced the proud fortress to rubble and ashes. The castle remained as ruins until it was rebuilt in the 1870s.

◄ OLD HALF-TIMBERED, gabled houses frame the Marktplatz of Cochem with its Martinsbrunnen and the Baroque Rathaus. Behind it the steeple of St. Martin rises up. Destroyed in the last weeks of World War II, the steeple which was crowned by a grandiose Baroque hood, was rebuilt after the war. Only the choir remained of the Late Gothic core of the church.

◄ KOBLENZ. A good 2,000 years ago the Romans built a fortress in the Middle Rhine Valley which they called Castrum ad Confluentes (castle at the confluence). This refers to the confluence of the Rhine and the Moselle. The narrow tongue of land between the two rivers is named Deutsches Eck ("German corner") after the house of the Knights of the Teutonic Order ("Ritter des Deutschen Ordens"), which was built at the beginning of the 13th century in what is today Koblenz. The famous memorial stands opposite the massive fortress Ehrenbreitstein.

◄ THE MONUMENT OF KAISER WILHELM has stood on the Deutsches Eck in Koblenz since 1897 and has at times been used as a memorial to German unity. It was recently restored after being damaged during World War II. Truly ornamental? Opinions are divided on this. The French poet Guillaume Apollinaire called the monumental figure on horseback a "revoltingly gigantic monument," and for Kurt Tucholsky it was a "stone punch with a fist"...

◀◀ WIESBADEN. The Hessian Staatstheater ("state theatre") in the state capital of Wiesbaden, a real temple to the muses and architectural highlight of the spa resort designed in the 19th/20th centuries. The thermal springs of the city in the Taunus hills, which were used for cures and wellness before the Roman period already and which are among the hottest springs in Central Europe, remain unseen.

◀◀ FRANKFURT. Guests from the USA see a familiar sight after their flight across the Atlantic and landing in Frankfurt Airport in "Mainhattan". In no other German city are the skyscrapers as close together and as high as in the banking, stock market and trade fair centre Frankfurt am Main.

▲ HISTORIC FRANKFURT is almost lost under the masses of cement, glass and steel. One of the traditional sites is the Römerberg with the Römer, the old Rathaus of the city on the Main River, the fountain of justice and some mostly reconstructed gabled houses. Nearby is the Paulskirche, a nucleus of German unity and democracy. The German national assembly of 1848/49 was held here.

◀ JOHANN WOLFGANG VON GOETHE. The leading poet Johann Wolfgang von Goethe was a genuine son of Frankfurt. He was born in 1749 in the street Am Großen Hirschgraben and grew up there. His birthplace is furnished with reproductions of his time and serves as a museum today.

◀ AT THE FOOT of the 250m/273yd tall Messeturm in Frankfurt am Main the "Hammering Man" hammers away. The sculpture by US American artist Jonathan Borofsky is seen as a symbol for work and enterprise. There are similar sculptures in other world cities.

▼ HEIDELBERG. Many people have lost their hearts in this city on the lower Neckar River. Not a few because of the Renaissance castle which is still one of the grandiose monuments between North Sea and Alps despite being in ruins. Others because of the famous barrel in the castle cellar which promises endless pleasure in the far more than 200,000 litres/52,800 US gallons of wine it holds (if it were full); but most people lost their hearts to the harmony of nature and culture that have made Heidelberg itself a work of art.

▼ ▼ THE NECKAR (here at Heidelberg) may not be equal to "Father Rhine", but it has a certain atmosphere at times in which you could lose your heart.

▼ THE BEST VIEW of this work of art which was created by man and by nature is from the Philosophenweg which runs high above Heidelberg along the right-hand banks of the Neckar on the slopes of the Heiligenberg.

▼ MANNHEIM. Colourful flowerbeds, sparkling waterworks and in the background the 60m/65yd high water tower built in the 1880s. The structure which serves mundane purposes is the landmark of Mannheim, a city which could be called the "square metropolis" because of its checkerboard-like city centre.

► IN THE WINTER of 1784 Heidelberg experienced the worst natural catastrophe in the long history of the city. Floods and drifting ice destroyed the vital bridge over the Neckar, which is called the "Alte Brücke" or "Karl-Theodor-Brücke" today after being rebuilt. The two towers of the bridge gate in front of the old city were part of the 15th century city wall and were later redesigned in Baroque style.

◀◀ SCHLOSS KARLSRUHE is the pivot point of the fan-shaped network of streets which lead to the Grand Duke's residence. There are numerous sculptures on the castle square, including many lightly clad female figures. Do the judges of the highest German courts who make their decisions in Karlsruhe condemn this? Certainly not.

◀ PFORZHEIM which lies on the edge of the Black Forest, is known far beyond German borders as the city of gold and precious jewelry. The modern Marktplatz (market place) with its charming waterworks and the Neue Rathaus (new town hall) of 1973, where a glockenspiel plays several times a day, is well suited for this.

◀ LUDWIGSBURG. The supposedly so thrifty Swabians certainly did not spare expenses when building the Residenzschloss in the "Swabian Versailles." With 452 rooms in 18 buildings the Ludwigsburger Schloss is one of the largest preserved German Baroque castles.

▼ BRUCHSAL. Feudal grandiose Baroque buildings in the lowlands of the upper Rhine River as well, where the princebishop of Speyer laid the foundation of a residence in Bruchsal befitting his position anno 1722. The building was completely destroyed in World War II and rebuilt in 1975, with the staircase designed by Balthasar Neumann, which is considered to be the "crown of all staircases."

◄◄ **FREIBURG.** Half-timbering and red sandstone give the old city of Freiburg its charming appearance. The cultural centre of the Breisgau at the foot of the Black Forest has in its Münster Unserer Lieben Frau a work of exquisite German architecture. Construction began around 1120 in Romanesque style, the choir completed in 1515 is in Late Gothic style.

◄◄ **THE BLACK FOREST.** The costumes of the Black Forest are as varied as the wooded, mountainous landscape. The hats decorated with red pompoms which have become a worldwide symbol, actually belong to only three communities in the central Black Forest. Here in Wolfach-Kirnbach the "Black Forest maid" is wearing the long-established costume. The men appear much more reserved in their large black hats.

▲ **SCHAUINSLAND.** Down in the Markgräfler Land the vineyards, then the forested mountains and in the highest regions expansive meadows like on the Schauinsland (about 1,300m/4,265ft above sea level), Freiburg's local mountain with beautiful views. In the winter the storm beaten beech trees bend under the weight of snow and frost.

◄ **MARKGRÄFLER LAND.** Fertile loess soil, a warm climate and not last the skill of the winegrowers make the Markgräfler Land to one of the best known wine regions of Baden and all of Germany. The Chasselas grape is especially prized at the foot of the southern Black Forest.

◄ **ST. TRUDPERT MONASTERY.** The Christianising of the southern Black Forest began from Kloster St. Trudpert in the broad Münstertal in the 7th century by Irish monks. The Baroque church with the beautiful onion-shaped dome is the landmark of the former Benedictine monastery.

▼ STUTTGART. The Staatsgalerie in Stuttgart, whose exhibits can be admired in a classicistic older building and a new modern building, enjoys an internationally excellent reputation. The gallery was started already in 1843 by King Wilhelm I. of Württemberg as a "museum of visual arts." The spectrum of exhibited works goes from paintings of the Swabian School to the Dutch, Italians and French to contemporary graphic art.

▼▼ SUMMER IN THE CITY. It can be uncomfortably warm and sticky in the summer in Stuttgart's valley basin. Street cafes with umbrella-covered tables and shady arcades like here in the Geißstraße are popular then.

▶▼ THE MERCEDES BENZ MUSEUM is the core of the Mercedes Benz World opened in May of 2006 in Stuttgart-Bad Cannstadt, the modern customer service centre of the international corporation. The avantgarde building holds rich collections which impressively document the history of Mercedes Benz.

▼▶ THE SCHLOSSPLATZ in Stuttgart, a Baroque garden with a fountain, music pavilion and commemorative column, is one of the most beautiful squares in Europe. It is flanked by the Neue Schloss to the east. Building on this grandiose residence for the dukes of Württemberg was begun in the middle of the 18th century.

▶ THE BRONZE STATUE OF CONCORDIA, the ancient Roman goddess of concord, stands on top of the commemorative column about 30m/33yd high above the Schlossplatz in Stuttgart. It was created to commemorate the 25th anniversary of the reign of King Wilhelm I. of Württemberg and was made in 1841 to 1846 by the court master builder Johann Michael Knapp.

◄◄ **KONSTANZ.** The "Imperia" guards the harbour entrance of Constance in truly majestic pose. The mobile sculpture which rotates with the help of a motor, has been standing at Lake Constance since 1993. Its creator, the sculptor Peter Lenk, wanted to remind the public symbolically (and satirically) of the Council of Constance (1414–18). "Imperia" holds two little figures in her hands symbolising the secular and the clerical powers of the time. They are half-naked, just as "Imperia" herself – alluding to the fact that the Konzil in those days also attracted around 1,000 prostitutes...

▲ **THE "MEERSBURG"**, which is surrounded by vineyards, above Lake Constance is Germany's oldest still occupied castle. The massive Dagobertsturm in the center was probably built already in the 12th century; the four round towers on the corners were added in the 16th century. The most famous resident of the picturesque castle is the poet Annette von Droste-Hülshoff (1797–1848) who spent the last years of her life here.

◄ **MAINAU.** A great variety of plants flourish in the mild climate of Lake Constance on the "flower island" of Mainau, even those from subtropical and tropical zones.

▼ **FRIEDRICHSHAFEN** on Lake Constance is permanently tied to the history of airships. The Zeppelin Museum at the harbour documents the development of the quiet giants of the air; but it commemorates Count Ferdinand von Zeppelin above all.

▼ REGENSBURG. Camp of Roman legions, seat of Bavarian dukes, often location of Imperial assemblies, seat of the perpetual Imperial diet – only a few of the historical roles of the city whose center along with the neighbouring Stadtamhof have been on the UNESCO World Heritage list since 2006. Hardly any other city in Germany has been able to keep the character of the high Middle Ages like Regensburg.

▼▼ THE NEUE WAAGE on the Haidplatz in Regensburg used to be a pub for men, then it was the city weighing office. The core of the tower, in which the reformer Melanchthon debated Johannes Eck in 1541, a strong critic of the Reformation, comes from the 13th century.

▼ THE STEINERNE BRÜCKE with a total of 16 arches on mighty pillars has spanned the Danube in Regensburg for more than 800 years. Construction of the bridge began anno 1135; it was completed in 1146.

▼▼ THE DOM OF ST. PETER, home of the world famous boys' choir "Regensburger Domspatzen", is a main work of Gothicism in Bavaria and one of its largest churches. It holds about 7,000 people and contains many valuable works of art for admiring eyes,

▶ WALHALLA. Immediately below Donaustauf the startled traveler sees a work of classical antiquity: a Greek temple, with massive steps leading down to the Danube. Bavarian King Ludwig I. commissioned the Valhalla, Leo von Klenze built it in 1830–42 based on ancient models of the Acropolis in Athens. The monarch wanted the white marble building to be a "German Hall of Fame", so today the hall contains busts of German "heroes", from Konrad Adenauer to Carl Friedrich Gauß.

◀◀ ROTHENBURG. Just as Switzerland symbolises unique landscapes, Rothenburg is the symbol of a city with beautiful medieval buildings. There are other cities in Germany which claim this status. But the original Rothenburg ob der Tauber, as seen here at the picturesque Plönlein with Siebersturm, is of course the most beautiful.

◀ IN NÜRNBERG, "Treasury of the German Empire", building monuments from its long history crowd close together: the castle, St. Sebaldus, St. Lorenz, the Rathaus, the "Schöne Brunnen" in the Hauptmarkt...

◀ THE NÜRNBERGER CHRISTKINDLESMARKT is the main attraction of the Franconian city not only for children. During Advent, scents of the inimitable Lebkuchen (gingerbread), delicious sausages, steaming mulled wine and cool, pleasant beer fill the air.

▼ THE HANDWERKERHOF between the Königstor and the Frauentor is reminiscent of Nürnberg's long tradition as "city of craftsmen". From glass painters to doll makers to pewter makers, many branches of craftsmanship are represented. Of course, there is also a bakery for Lebkuchen, a pub for sausages and a wine bar.

◄◄ SCHLOSS NEUSCHWANSTEIN above Schwangau in the Ostallgäu: Famous art historians generally only give a few lines of text to the fairy castle, on which construction was begun in 1867 and which was modeled after the Wartburg, as if it were an embarrassment. But the castle which was built by the Bavarian King Ludwig II., is an important document: of German Historicism and of an emotionally torn personality, which fled from the present into the past.

◄ LINDERHOF CASTLE. A park with beautiful waterworks surrounds Schloss Linderhof near Ettal. Here King Ludwig II. was inspired by the Rococo spirit and style. The other-worldly dreamer preferred to live in this grandiose building which was embedded in magnificent Alpine scenery.

◄ HOHENSCHWANGAU. St. Peter supplies the fitting cloud background for Schloss Hohenschwangau near Schwangau. It was built in 1837 on the foundations of a castle in Neogothic style by Crown Prince Maximilian, the later King Max II. of Bavaria. The interior is decorated with grandiose wall paintings and costly furnishings.

▼ KÖNIGSSEE AND ST. BARTHOLOMÄ. For most of the passengers the quiet boat ride across the Königssee in the Berchtesgadener Alps ends on the peninsula of St. Bartholomä. On the peninsula at the foot of the steep cliffs of the Kleine Watzmann the Alpine farmers built a pilgrimage chapel dedicated to their patron saint St. Bartholomäus already in the 12th century.

Unser komplettes Programm:

www.bruckmann.de

Product Management: Dr. Reinhard Pietsch, Susanne Caesar
Typography & Layout: Dr. Alex Klubertanz, Munich
Editing: Dr. Alex Klubertanz, Munich
Translation: Barbara Schmidt-Runkel, Rottenburg
Text: Dr. Peter Göbel, Mücke-Atzenhain
Repros: Scanner Service, Verona
Cover Design: Anna Katavic, and use of a photograph of the Huber Picture Agency
Cartography: Kartengrafik Thomas Vogelmann, Mannheim
Production: Bettina Schippel, Christine Herzer
Printed in Spain by Tallers Grafics Soler S.A.

All facts contained were carefully researched by the author in consideration of the latest information available and fact-checked by the publisher. However, legal responsibility may not be inferred. We are always grateful for advice and suggestions. The address for these is:

Bruckmann Verlag
Postfach 80 02 40
D–81602 München
E-Mail: lektorat@bruckmann.de

Front Cover: Neuschwanstein castle
Back Cover: Hiddensee; Potsdam; Hamburg
Pages 6–7: Springflowers Allgäu, Page 93: Chiemsee

All cover illustrations, as well those in the text, are by Bildagentur Huber, Garmisch-Partenkirchen.

BILDAGENTUR
HUBER

Updated reprint
2010,© 2007 Bruckmann Verlag GmbH, Munich
ISBN 978-3-7654-4608-5